MARK TULLY

BEYOND PURDAH

D1324528

PENGUIN BOOKS

PENGUIN BOOKS

Published by the Penguin Group. Penguin Books Ltd, 27 Wrights Lane, London w8 5TZ, England. Penguin Books USA Inc., 375 Hudson Street, New York, New York 10014, USA. Penguin Books Australia Ltd, Ringwood, Victoria, Australia. Penguin Books Canada Ltd, 10 Alcorn Avenue, Toronto, Ontario, Canada M4V 3B2. Penguin Books (NZ) Ltd, 182 – 190 Wairau Road, Auckland 10, New Zealand · Penguin Books Ltd, Registered Offices: Harmondsworth, Middlesex, England · These extracts are from *The Heart of India* by Mark Tully, published by Viking 1995. This edition published 1996 · Copyright © Mark Tully, 1995. All rights reserved · The moral right of the author has been asserted · Typeset by Rowland Phototypesetting Ltd, Bury St Edmunds, Suffolk. Printed in England by Clays Ltd, St Ives plc ·

CONTENTS

The Barren Woman of Balramgaon

The water in the drain in front of the small temple of Shiva was normally a dismal muddy brown, but today it was a bright, cheerful purple. The dog stretched out on the temple platform had scarlet and yellow patches added to the brown and white the gods had given him. The temple platform itself was stained with green and scarlet. It was Holi in the village of Balramgaon – the spring festival when everyone and everything is smeared with coloured powder or dowsed with dyed water. The Yadavs who dominated the village had just finished singing a *faag*, or special Holi song, in honour of Shiva and were now moving on to their next destination, the house of the primary-school teacher.

The men chatted excitedly to each other as they walked. One young man, whose hair had been stained even blacker than usual, said, 'Now we've got to sing a *faag* of Krishna. After all, that's what Holi is about: Braj, the home of Lord Krishna.'

Another, wearing a cotton cap with 'Happy Holi' embroidered on it, laughed and said, 'Yes! Let's celebrate Krishna. He stole the clothes of the milkmaids while they were bathing at Vrindavan. Let's celebrate that.'

An old man with a yellow stain on his white beard coloured green, did not approve of that remark. Wagging his finger, he said, 'We Yadavs don't want anything like that on Holi. We don't get drunk and run off into the fields with other men's women. That's work for the Bhangis and Chamars.'

'More's the pity,' the younger man replied.

The ragged group walked on past empty houses with *charpoys* turned up on the verandas. No one was going to laze on them today. Children wearing only tattered underpants, their faces smeared with an assortment of colours, ran about with water-pistols shaped like fishes and plastic plungers fixed in bottles of noxious-looking coloured liquid, spraying anyone who didn't manage to get out of their range. Two old farmers hobbled along with the help of long bamboo staves. Only the cows and sleek black buffaloes tethered in front of the houses were unmoved by the excitement of the festival.

The schoolmaster's brick house, plastered with pale-brown mud, stood in a small grove. Two tall *neem* trees provided shade for his small courtyard. Yellow oleanders were in flower, as were red cannas and purple bougainvillaea. Holi was the season for flowers, especially red flowers that were used to make the colouring smeared everywhere. The schoolmaster stood on the veranda to greet the *faag* party. He embraced each man three times, saying, 'Holi greetings,' and then asked them to sit down. Sweet pastries known as *gujias* and salty snacks were produced. Cigarettes, *bidis* and matches were passed round on a metal tray.

The *faag* party sat under the thatched eaves of the veranda. They were divided into two groups. Chote Lal Yadav, who had seen more than eighty Holis, put his hands on the shoulders of two men and lowered himself gingerly. Everyone looked towards him. He raised his arm, pointed at the men opposite and started singing:

> 'My snake-lord is sleeping – Krishna, run away from here.
> My snake-lord's a killer – Krishna, go there and he'll bite.
> My snake-lord is sleeping here –
> Sweet child, run from Kali's lair.
> Hah, hah, hah, hah!'

The refrain was taken up by the rest of his group, singing at the tops of their voices to make themselves heard above the frenzied beat of the drums, the clashing of tambourines and the clanging of cymbals.

Then the other group repeated the refrain, leaning forward and pointing aggressively at their opponents to give the impression that they were singing even louder. Chote Lal Yadav's jaw sagged as he sat, silently waiting for the chance to come back at them. When it came he led his group in singing:

> 'Said child Krishna, "Go and wake him.
> It's him I've come to nail.
> I'm going to kill your snake-lord
> And play within his lair." '

When the first song was over, Ram Lakhan Yadav, a man of about thirty who had been sitting at the back, taking no part in the *faag*, rose and picked his way through the singers towards the gap between the two groups where the percussionists were sitting. He was carrying a pair of cymbals.

Chote Lal Yadav said, '*Arre bhai*, sit down, we don't need any more cymbals. Two are quite enough. If you too come in now, we won't be able to make ourselves heard above all the banging and clashing.'

A young man, Hoshiar Singh, sneered, 'Get out of here, Ram Lakhan. Holi's the season for cutting the crop – and where's your crop? Don't you know how to plough? Something wrong with the seed? Didn't you irrigate the field? What's the problem? People like you bring us bad luck. We'll have poor crops this year if you play Holi with us. Wait until your house produces some children before trying to play those cymbals.'

Ram Lakhan pulled the young man to his feet and punched him in the face. Before a full-scale fight could develop the singers were on their feet, pinning back the arms of the two men. Ram Lakhan was frog-marched off the veranda and given a parting kick to see him on his way.

In the small inner courtyard of the house next to Ram Lakhan's his wife was standing against the wall watching women pressing the pastry for *gujias* into moulds and frying *papadums* and *kachoris*. A child darted to the pile of freshly cooked *gujias* and stuffed one into his mouth. His young mother caught him up in her arms, hugged him and said, 'What will we do if you go on like that? The men will be very angry if there are not enough *gujias* for everyone who comes to the house today. They will smack you if I tell them what the problem is.'

There was a tussle going on in another corner between one of the brothers of the house and his younger sister-in-law. She was trying to stop him pouring a pot of coloured water over her, but let go of the pot for one moment to prevent the border of her sari from slipping off her head and found herself drenched with yellow dye.

Ram Lakhan's wife thought, 'I have no brother-in-law to play Holi with, no children to hug. I look like all these women here. I've got the same gold nosepin, the same bangles, the same silver anklets. I wear the red *sindoor* of a married woman in my hair. But really I'm nothing like them because I have no children, and there's no family in our house.'

Rani and Sima, two of the younger wives of the family, came over to her. Rani asked, 'Why don't you have any colour on your face or your sari? Doesn't anyone play Holi with you?'

Sima giggled and said, 'Nobody plays Holi with a barren woman. It brings bad luck.'

Ram Lakhan's wife stared silently at the ground.

Sima poked her in the ribs and asked, 'Have you been sitting under our mango trees? They should be flowering now, but they aren't, and people say that if a barren woman sits in a mango grove, the trees won't flower.'

Both giggled like the schoolchildren they really were, and Rani said, 'Come on, we are wasting our time. Her mouth is closed as tight as her womb.'

Ram Lakhan's wife walked around the edge of the courtyard, her head turned towards the wall, until she reached the front door. No one noticed her going. It was as if she had never come to play Holi with her neighbours.

The Yadavs of Balramgaon paid calls on each other until late that night. Ram Lakhan wondered whether he should call on the man who had insulted him. It was said to be particularly important at Holi to go to the homes of people you were not on speaking terms with, but he couldn't face the possibility of another insult, so he stayed inside his room. When his wife came to the door and announced that food had been cooked, he said, 'How can I eat food when all day I have had to eat the insults of my own *biradari*? You eat. I'm not coming out.'

Ram Lakhan's wife went back to the corner of the courtyard where she had her kitchen and tried to eat a little herself, but she too had no appetite. She did not have the energy to wash the pans in which the vegetables had been cooked. She squatted against the wall, looking up at the cloudless night sky, bright with a full moon and countless stars, and thinking of her own noisy family home where a new child had always just arrived and her great-grandparents seemed set to live for ever. What a stark contrast to this silent, lonely house where only she and Ram Lakhan lived.

The family she had married into had a tradition of dying young, and Ram Lakhan had been an only child.

The silence was broken by a shout from her husband's room. 'Come here, you. I want to talk to you.'

She covered her head, stood up, walked slowly across the court-yard and stood in the doorway. Her husband shouted, 'Come in,' but did not get up. He ordered her brusquely to squat on the floor at the end of the *charpoy* on which he was lying.

Turning on his side and looking towards the wall, Ram Lakhan said in a surly voice, 'Because of you, my Holi has been terrible. Everyone else joking about red colour for a woman's monthly blood, fertility, Krishna and the milkmaids, and I've had to eat insults about your infertility. I've had to eat blows too, and I've been kicked up the backside. They wouldn't even let me take part in *faag* in case I brought bad luck to their crops.'

His wife said, 'Do you think mine has been any better? Do you think I haven't eaten insults? The two youngest daughters-in-law next door, just children, they spoke to me as though I was some old hag, some servant they could behave with as badly as they liked. Now I come home only to be ill-treated by you.'

'What do you mean? It's my right to speak to you as I like. Now not only do I get no respect in the village, I don't even get it at home. My own wife answers me back. Am I a man or just a pair of pyjamas? I am not going to endure another Holi like this one. Either you produce a child this year, or I will send you back home and take another woman.' Rani started to sob quietly. 'Don't start crying again. You always try that one and then you turn my mind, and I am lost. This time I really mean it. There must be something you can do.'

'I'm crying because it's so sad. We live much better than most others in this village. You know how to speak to me so well at night, whereas other women tell me how rough their men are sometimes, but still it's no good because we can't produce children.'

Ram Lakhan was easily moved by his wife. Perhaps because of their loneliness they had become very close. She was certainly not just a cook and a housekeeper. She had a fair complexion and green eyes, rare in Belramgaon. As a child she had carried brass pots of water on her head every day. Balancing them had given her a lithe hip movement which could still arouse Ram Lakhan when he watched her walking.

He sat up, swung his feet over the end of the *charpoy* and started to undo her hair. It flowed down her back – shining and black. He ran his fingers through it and said, 'I don't want to lose you. I know that you are much better than any other man's wife in this village, but we can't go on like this. Something has to be done.'

His wife scrambled up on to the *charpoy* and pulled him down beside her, saying, 'This is the only way to produce babies.'

After making love the couple lay on their backs, looking up at the fan wobbling hazardously on its stem as it stirred the warm night air. Rani said lazily, 'I've heard that it's not always the woman who is infertile. It can be the man, and then there are some medicines to help with that. I have been to the family-planning clinic, and they say there is no reason why I can't have children. Perhaps it would be a good idea if you went to see a doctor.'

'But you know there's nothing wrong with me. I've just shown you again that there's no shortage of seed in me. The doctors don't know everything. It's obvious that it's you who are barren.'

Rani, realizing that there was no point in trying to persuade 7 him any further, turned on her side, saying, 'Well, then, all that's left is praying to the gods for the gift of children.'

The gods did not oblige, but the Pradhan didn't like quarrels among the Yadavs as they threatened to divide his community, which was the source of his political strength. Unless all the Yadavs voted together he would not be re-elected. So he called Ram Lakhan and Hoshiar Singh to his house. He said to Ram Lakhan, 'Fights sometimes happen in every community, but why did you have to have a fight on Holi of all days?'

Ram Lakhan replied, 'He insulted me. He said I couldn't join the *faag* because I was childless and that would bring bad luck to everyone. He was obscene too, making lewd remarks about my not knowing how to sow my seed.'

'Is that true?' the Pradhan asked Hoshiar Singh.

'Well, I meant it only as a joke. Everyone makes jokes about that sort of thing on Holi. There was no need for his brain to get so hot. He should have been able to take it.'

'No man should be asked to tolerate insults to his wife, whether she is barren or not. In the old days I would have called a meeting of the caste council and asked them to impose *hookah pani bund* on you to teach you how to behave and what jokes are proper and what are not. Now, unfortunately, the rules are more lenient. If we are to hold the community together, we can't be too strict. I suggest that you apologize and let it be known in the village that you were in the wrong.'

Hoshiar Singh clasped his hands and said, 'All right, Pradhanji, I have nothing against Ram Lakhan. I don't know why I lost my head. Perhaps it was the *bhang*. I have to admit that I had drunk a glass and that was wrong too.'

The Pradhan laughed and said, 'All right, we will overlook that too this time. Young men will be young men. Now embrace Ram Lakhan, and let's hear no more about it.'

So Ram Lakhan's honour was restored, and he was able to rejoin the group of Yadavs who gathered at the Pradhan's house each evening to discuss everything from village gossip to national politics. The elders still passed a hookah round; the younger men smoked *bidis*, or cigarettes. There was no liquor – the Pradhan strongly disapproved of that because drinking also led to quarrels.

One evening they were discussing the rice crop. It looked as if it would be particularly good that year. The Pradhan said, 'Now that we have a Yadav Chief Minister in Lucknow there's been no problem over bank loans to buy seeds, no shortage of fertilizers, and we have even been able to see that the water reaches our canal, so we have every reason to be thankful.'

A farmer who, by virtue of his years, was rather less respectful to the Pradhan than most of the Yadavs, wagged his finger angrily at him saying, 'Satpal, what are you talking about? You, the Pradhan of my *biradari*, are praising the politicians for a good harvest. In my days the young men would have gone to give thanks to Guru Gorakhnath at the *mela* in the temple at Gorakhpur, but nowadays the politicians think they are gods, and people like you only encourage them by giving them credit for everything. It's shameful. If the Chief Minister came here, you wouldn't just touch his feet, you'd lie down on the ground in front of him. Where's your pride as a Yadav?'

Hoshiar Singh, anxious to re-establish himself in the Pradhan's favour, said, 'Old man, you don't understand these times. Our Pradhan has to be a politician too, otherwise we would get nothing. Everything comes from *sifarish*, and if you don't have contacts, you can't do *sifarish*. The days of the gods are over. We have to live on this earth, on the soil of this village.'

But the Pradhan was not so pleased by this defence as Hoshiar Singh had hoped. He was himself a religious man, and so he didn't want anyone to commit the sin of hubris on his behalf. At the same time he wanted to avoid a split between the elderly and the young in his community. He turned on Hoshiar Singh and said, 'You fool. Don't show disrespect to the gods or to your elders. That's the whole trouble nowadays: the young have no respect for the past. You think everything started from the time you first went to the barber for a shave. I think some of you should go to Gorakhpur this year to show your respect for God and put an end to this arrogance. I would suggest that you go, Hoshiar Singh, and you can take Ram Lakhan with you, so that he can pray for help with his problem – and you make sure there's no fighting this time.'

Hoshiar Singh and Ram Lakhan were left with no choice, so they and three other young Yadavs spent a cold night on the train to the town of Gorakhpur in the middle of January. When they reached the shrine of holy man Guru Gorakhnath they found there was a large, crowded and noisy fair outside the temple gates. The young men decided to see what it had to offer before going on to fulfil their more solemn purpose. At the entrance of the fair barbers sat waiting to shave the heads of young children brought to pay their respects to Guru Gorakhnath. A man was having his luxuriant moustache trimmed. He held a mirror in one hand to make sure the barber didn't cut it back too far but at the same time toned down its arrogant assertion of manhood sufficiently to avoid insulting the god he had come to worship.

In the fairground they found the usual mixture of sacred and secular which goes with almost all Indian religious occasions. There were women sitting cross-legged on the ground behind piles of orange, bright-red, shocking-pink and bilious-green powder. There were stalls selling calendars with pictures of the gods. A few young women, revealing the smooth brown skin between their blouses and their lowslung saris had somehow found their way into this pantheon.

Bharat photographers offered the opportunity of portraits set against various backgrounds. They could make it appear that customers had been photographed at the Kaaba in Mecca, in a Hindu temple or at the architecturally much admired new Baha'i temple in Delhi. They could also give the impression that they had been sitting with the film star Sri Devi in a room filled with all modern conveniences. Outside balloons and bubbles blown by the sellers of bubble mixture floated in the air. A vendor of flutes repeated monotonously the same few notes in the hope of persuading customers that it was not too difficult to play his instruments. All the rich variety of Indian cuisine was on offer. The young Yadavs made their way to a café and ordered white crunchy sweets called *khaja mithai*. Hoshiar Singh said, 'After this let's see the side-shows, so that we can enjoy ourselves, before we go to the temple to keep the Pradhan happy.'

As they made their way towards a giant wheel crowned with the Indian flag, they passed an exhausted mother reclining against the white cotton bags in which she had brought pots, pans and all the other necessities of a long family outing. She held a baby in her lap, and two small girls tugged at her *sari*, impatiently urging her to spend more of the family's scant resources. An old man was snoring peacefully, the urge to sleep having triumphed over the discordant music blaring from the side-shows and other entertainments. A young couple were investigating the contents of their tiffin carrier.

The Yadavs had a ride on a gigantic swing, shaped like a Viking boat. They took pot-shots at prizes with air-guns whose sights had been deliberately distorted. They stared at a tent advertised as 'Saajan Disco Dance Party'. It was topped by a ten-foot cut-out of a lady whose scant pink sari had slipped down to her buttocks and revealed almost all of her legs. Ram Lakhan refused to countenance entering that tent, so they went on to a freak show which promised a snake with the head of a woman but decided that it hardly fitted in with the sacred purpose of their visit. Then they came across a young man standing by a tricycle van. He was surrounded by a crowd of men. They guffawed as he bellowed through his megaphone, 'Sand-lizard oil! Rub it on and you'll feel the difference. Put your cock in at Kanpur, you'll take it out at Gorakhpur. One bottle only ten rupees, and what a surprise you'll give the ladies!'

One of the crowd shouted, 'How do we know?'

'I've told you. Try for yourself. Have you ever seen the Qutab Minar tower in Delhi, hundreds of feet high and built of solid stone? How do you think they got that up in those days, years ago when they didn't have scaffolding? They didn't. They built it flat along the ground, rubbed sand-lizard oil on it and it stood up all on its own. Sand-lizard, the oil for men. It's only ten rupees a bottle, ten rupees a bottle. Roll up, roll up. Ten rupees a bottle, to put bone in your prick. Do you want a cock, or would you like a spade? Do you want to screw, or do you really want to make the grade?'

One man was pushed forward by his friends, handed over a ten-rupee note and hurriedly shoved a bottle of oil into the pocket of his *kurta*. That broke the barrier of reserve. The salesman crammed ten-rupee notes into a shabby black bag, while his assistant handed out the bottles.

Hoshiar Singh said, 'I'll give it a go,' and pushed his way through the crowd surrounding the salesman. As he handed over a ten-rupee note he asked whether there was any medicine to produce children.

The salesman produced a packet from the cupboard fixed to his cycle-rickshaw, saying, 'With these pills you can get milk out of a bullock and puppies out of a barren bitch.'

Hoshiar Singh handed over another ten-rupee note, went back to his colleagues and gave the packet to Ram Lakhan, saying, 'Don't be angry. You never know. They might work.'

Ram Lakhan was not amused, but he didn't want to draw attention to himself. So he took the pills and walked away, saying, 'I've had enough of this. There's a long queue to get into the temple. If we don't stop fooling around, we won't get to see Guru Gorakhnath today.'

The queue was moving slowly across the park towards the white temple with its three tall *shikaras*, or towers. The devotees were penned between two wooden fences to keep them in line. As the Yadavs joined the queue a well-dressed man was arguing with the sub-inspector in charge of the police party, whose job it was to ensure that everyone joined the queue and no devotee crossed the rope barrier and walked straight up to the temple. The man protested, 'I'm a government servant. I am allowed to go straight into the temple.'

The sub-inspector growled, 'No one is allowed past this barrier. Those are my orders.'

'But you can't expect a man in my position to stand in a queue like this, especially as I have my wife and children with me.'

13

'There are plenty of wives and children in the queue. Get in line or get out.'

The Yadavs stopped to join the crowd which was gathering to witness this altercation. Hoshiar Singh said, 'You have spoken exactly right, Inspector Sahib. These government servants, they think they are the owners of India. They need to be shown something.'

Then, turning to his friends, he asked in a loud voice, 'Have you seen his wife?'

'What do you mean?' another Yadav replied.

'Look at the gold around her neck, look at the gold on her arms, look at the gold on her fingers. A government officer doesn't need to come to this festival. He takes enough bribes to afford to go to Tirupati where you offer gold and jewels. He's come here only because he's mean. He's heard that Guru Gorakhnath will listen to your prayers for just a bag of rice.'

The crowd roared with laughter. The civil servant walked off as quickly as the small modicum of decorum he retained would allow, leaving his wife to drag their two young children away as best she could. The police sub-inspector said, 'Bastards. Shameless people. They think everyone is going to touch their feet, and then, when they are challenged, they don't have the courage to face up to it. Anyway you certainly made an owl out of that one.' Then, turning to face the crowd, he said, 'I'm going to take this lot to the top of the queue, just to show that I am the law around here. Even bastard government servants have to listen to me.'

So the Yadavs found themselves being led through the park to the pillared portico of the temple. No one dared to object to the sub-inspector when he inserted them at the front of the queue. Behind them stood a group of farmers wearing brightly coloured turbans and speaking a dialect from the Rajasthan desert the Yadavs couldn't understand. There were also men wearing side-caps set at jaunty angles, who had come across the nearby border with the Himalayan state of Nepal. Ram Lakhan said, 'I thought this was a local festival for people like us from the east, but people seem to have come from everywhere.'

Hoshiar Singh replied, 'I have heard that Lord Gorakhnath was a very powerful *yogi*. That's, I suppose, why people come here from all over India. Look behind you. There are some Bengalis wearing *dhotis* so long that I can't understand why they don't trip over them. People know that a *yogi* is much more likely to do their work than that bastard government officer I saw off. That's why they have faith in Lord Gorakhnath. Maybe he will do your work too,' he said to Ram Lakhan.

'I thought you'd given the Pradhan an assurance that you would not tease me about that any more. Now you first go and buy me those pills, and then tell me what I have to ask from Lord Gorakh-nath. I don't want another fight. Why don't you leave me alone?'

'All right, all right. I accept. I only thought it might help. We all have problems, after all, and I will certainly ask Lord Gorakh-nath to solve mine.'

'You ask him to solve yours and leave me to ask him to solve mine.'

The priests controlling the temple were anxious that devotees should not spend too much time in front of the image of Guru Gorakhnath because the more pilgrims who passed through the temple the more wealth they contributed. So the queue moved forward through the temple hall at a steady pace, and Ram Lakhan soon reached the *sanctum sanctorum*. It was an alcove, separated from the rest of the temple by rails.

Coins, rice, marigolds and roses rained down on the marble floor in front of the image. Ram Lakhan pushed through the crowd to the rails, where he handed over a bag of rice and lentils and a red cardboard box. One priest filled the box with sweet *prasad*; another poured the rice and lentils on to the marble floor, where it was promptly swept into a mound, growing ever larger, on the side of the *sanctum sanctorum*. Ram Lakhan stared at the modern alabaster image, the size of a small man. Guru Gorakhnath sat cross-legged in a glass case set high enough for devotees to get a good look at him. He was not a god and he had no divine trappings, no extra arms or legs, no weapons, no conch shells, no discus. But his almond-shaped eyes were exaggerated, his face was supernaturally smooth and his lips were bright red. He was garlanded with marigolds and crowned with a double halo of small yellow bulbs. The outline of his red throne was also picked out by two strings of yellow lights.

It was not easy for Ram Lakhan to concentrate on his prayers. He was squeezed up against the rails by the pressure of the devotees behind him. One man next to him was being particularly troublesome by trying to make space to prostrate himself before Guru Gorakhnath. The priests and their acolytes kept on urging Ram Lakhan, not always too politely, to move on, but he stuck to his ground until he had spent what he believed was sufficient time, and had prayed with enough intensity, to convey his request to the *rishi*.

Ram Lakhan's wife had also been investigating the possibility of divine intervention. One of the older village midwives had told her of a Yadav lady who had suddenly produced a child after apparently being barren for nearly ten years. Ram Lakhan's wife said she would like to see her, and a meeting was arranged. When Ram Lakhan's wife entered the courtyard of the elderly lady, Sita Devi, she found her sitting alone in one corner. She asked Ram Lakhan's wife to sit beside her and said, 'I have managed to get rid of the other women because the midwife told me what you wanted to talk about, but we'd better be quick, otherwise they'll come back.'

Ram Lakhan's wife looked down at the ground and said softly, 'You know that I have been accused of being barren, as you were. The midwife told me that maybe you could say whether there was anything you did to have a child.'

'I was told by the midwife to go with another man just once or twice. She told me, "Go into the fields one night. It's probably your man's fault, not yours." But I didn't because I could not bring myself to do so, and anyhow I would have been ashamed to ask another man, although they're all such *badmashes* I am sure there would have been plenty to do the job. I wasn't that bad-looking, I can tell you.'

'So what did happen?'

'Well, I don't know that I know. I can give you only one piece of advice. If ever you hear that a wandering *sadhu* from Rishikesh has come to that small temple of Shiva by the Ganges, go and see him.'

'Which temple?'

'You know, the small one only about three miles from here. There is an *ashram* next to it, but the temple has nothing to do with it. I still go there to pray sometimes, and if I hear that the *sadhu* has come, I'll take you to him. Now go quickly. We don't want the whole village gossiping. Everyone will be able to guess why you have come to see me.'

A week or so before Ram Lakhan was due to go to Gorakhpur the midwife told his wife that Sita Devi wanted to see her again. Apparently the *sadhu* had arrived, but Sita Devi told Ram Lakhan's wife that the ceremony was very elaborate and she would have to stay in the temple all night. She had managed to do so by telling her family she was going back to see her parents. Ram Lakhan's wife decided it would be safest if she went while her husband was in Gorakhpur. It was unlikely that any neighbours would realize she had gone and, if they did, she could always use the same excuse as Sita Devi. The boy they employed to milk and feed the cattle wouldn't think anything of her absence. He'd assume she'd gone to someone else's house to gossip.

So, late in the afternoon when Ram Lakhan had left for Gorakhpur, his wife and Sita Devi set out to bathe in the Ganges. After about an hour they arrived at a small temple on a bank high above the sacred river, in the shade of a peepul tree. Although the bank was quite high, it flooded during the monsoon, and the waters had eroded the soil, leaving the tree's thick, gnarled roots exposed like giant pythons. The temple itself was built on a brick plinth. It had just one small *shikara* tower, surrounded on three sides by a veranda. A handsome *sadhu*, looking not much older than Ram Lakhan's wife, was sitting on the veranda opposite the Ganges. With him was a middle-aged woman and another holy man wearing a white shirt and a *dhoti*. He had thick spectacles askew on his nose and an undisciplined mop of curly black hair.

As they approached the temple Sita Devi said to Ram Lakhan's wife, 'The *sadhu* in the loincloth – he's the one I'm talking about.'

'But he looks far too young.'

'With *sadhus* you can never tell their age.'

It was the woman who first saw Sita Devi and Ram Lakhan's

wife climbing up the bank. She said to the *sadhu*, who was staring at the far bank of the Ganges, lost in contemplation, '*Babaji*, that village woman who was here the other day asking about having children – she's back. She's brought another woman with her, much younger. Maybe she's the one.'

The *sadhu* didn't turn his head but said, 'It's good.'

When the two Yadav women reached the temple veranda Sita Devi touched the *sadhu*'s feet, but he still didn't turn his head.

She said, '*Babaji*, I've brought the woman you promised to help.'

'It's good.'

The other holy man motioned the women to sit down and told them that the *sadhu* was meditating and should not be disturbed. After a short while the *sadhu* got up and, without saying a word to anyone, walked to the edge of the Ganges, took off his saffron *lungi* and walked into the river. He splashed water over himself noisily, then dipped into the water several times, submerging his whole body. When he emerged from the river he retied his *lungi*, climbed back to the temple and sat cross-legged again on his piece of sacking. He had a heart-shaped, intelligent face, which was lean but not pinched. His long, dank hair was piled on top of his head. A sparse beard straggled over his cheeks and chin, and there was no hair on his bare chest. After making himself comfortable he turned towards Sita Devi, gave her a broad grin and said, 'So you have come back and brought your friend. That's good.' Then, lowering his voice, he went on, 'All paths to God are one. If you drive ten kilometres from here, the name of the village will be different, but it will be the same earth. There are three questions. Where are we from? Why are we like this? And where are we going? Tantra answers these questions. It's a special knowledge, and just as the torch throws out light from inside, so does the wise man who is truly initiated into the left-hand path of Tantra, who can worship with all the five elements. They include what is forbidden to ordinary people, like meat, wine and sex.

'Why have you brought this woman to me?'

Sita Devi could not return his frank, knowing gaze. With her eyes cast down, she mumbled, 'You know, *Babaji*. To do what happened to me. To get Shiva to give her a baby.'

'You have faith because Shiva gave you a baby. Do you know that the great guru Shankaracharya revived a dead snake and then went on to the funeral of a king and brought him back to life too? If that's so, why shouldn't I bring life to the womb of this woman? But it must be remembered that we are not God. We worship Shiva because we do not have his powers. We cannot stop the world spinning. We can know what man has made, and then we are stupid enough to think we have understood what God has made. If you have faith in Shiva, then only I can help you. Go now and worship the *lingam*. She will assist you,' he added, pointing at the woman who had been sitting with him.

She took Sita Devi and Ram Lakhan's wife around the corner of the veranda to the small *sanctum sanctorum* where there was a black stone that had been taken from the Ganges, nobody knew when, to be worshipped as the *lingam* of Shiva. The *sadhu*'s disciple threw herself down, prostrate before the *lingam*, beat her head on the stone floor, repeating with mounting intensity, '*Jai bhole Shankar ki! Jai bhole Shankar ki!*' Ram Lakhan's wife and Sita Devi took marigolds and rose petals out of a cloth bag they had brought, sprinkled them on the *lingam*, placed a ten-rupee note under a coconut and sat with folded hands, waiting. Eventually the sound of '*Jai bhole Shankar ki*' got lower and lower, and the *sadhu*'s disciple rolled on to her back with her eyes staring vacantly at the ceiling of the shrine. Sita Devi and Ram Lakhan's wife went back to the *sadhu*.

'You have done the *puja* and given the *daan*?'

'Yes,' replied Sita Devi.

'Good, so you go now and leave your friend here. If you wish, you can come to collect her early tomorrow morning. Do you want someone to go with you for protection?'

'No. No one will attack an old woman like me.'

The *sadhu* chuckled and said, 'It wasn't always like that, was it?'

Sita Devi hid her face in the tail of her sari and left.

The *sadhu* then took Ram Lakhan's wife to a small room at the back of the temple. The other holy man brought in some wood, laid it in a pit in the centre of the room, dowsed it with *ghi* and set it alight. He then left. The *sadhu* sat in front of the fire opposite Ram Lakhan's wife. He recited mantras, from time to time throwing herbs into the fire. The sweet smell of the herbs and *ghi*, the low droning of the mantras, the flickering light from the fire all made Ram Lakhan's wife drowsy. The *sadhu* then poured what looked like milk into a metal glass and handed it to her, saying, 'This is Shankarji's *prasad*. Drink it.'

The milk was very sweet, just like the *thandai* served in the village on Holi. Very soon she started to feel strangely relaxed and euphoric, utterly at peace, almost removed from what was going on in the small, smoke-filled room. The *sadhu* said in a deep voice, 'You are the goddess – you are the female power, just as important as the male. If the two are not joined, there is no creation. Remember the destruction wrought by Shiva when the Goddess Sati burnt

herself alive because he had not been invited by her father to the
sacrifice? Remember what Sati and Shiva created when she was
reborn to life and they made love for a million years? Shiva can
come to you, but you must not have fear.' He repeated, 'You must
not have fear. You must not have fear,' again and again, his voice
becoming softer all the while.

Then the *sadhu* produced a human skull from under the wooden
platform on which he was sitting. Holding it up, he said, 'Tantrics
know no fear. That's why they like to worship in cremation
grounds to learn that nothing in this life is banned, and nothing
in this life is to be feared. I got this skull from a cremation
ground in the Himalayas, where a *sadhu* eats the flesh of the
dead.'

He threw powder into the fire to produce a blinding flash of
white light. The empty sockets of the skull stared at Ram Lakhan's
wife. She should have been terrified – Yadav women weren't even
allowed to attend cremations – but her strange sense of content-
ment was not in any way disturbed. She feared nothing. She could
do anything.

The *sadhu* said, 'When the power of Shiva and the power of
the Goddess come together I can overcome anything. Do you feel
a strange power overcoming you too?'

Ram Lakhan's wife nodded.

The *sadhu* lit a cigarette from the fire and puffed on it vigorously.
Then he put the cigarette in the mouth of the skull and said,
'Look. I can even make the dead come alive. I can bind spirits.
Watch him smoke.'

Ram Lakhan's wife, peering through the smoke of the fire at
the tip of the cigarette, saw it glow and dim, glow and dim, and
was convinced that the spirit of the skull was smoking. She stared

at it, fascinated. The *sadhu* came and sat beside her, looking deep into her eyes. She returned his gaze, although she would not normally have looked even at her husband so directly. Then the *sadhu* started to repeat, 'You must not have fear, you must not have fear.' She wanted to say, 'I haven't,' but somehow she couldn't speak. The *sadhu*'s words mesmerized her. The liturgy changed. The *sadhu* now repeated an invocation of Shiva and Parvati. Ram Lakhan's wife started to sway. The *sadhu* took her by the shoulders and laid her down by the fire, and she fell into a deep sleep.

Ram Lakhan's wife woke to find the *sadhu*'s woman shaking her, and saying, 'Get up, get up. You must bathe in the Ganges and then go back to your village.'

The woman helped her to stand. She felt dizzy. Her head was spinning, but the woman supported her. She picked up the cloth bag containing a spare sari which Ram Lakhan's wife had brought with her. The two walked uncertainly on to the veranda. Ram Lakhan's wife saw the *sadhu* in the same position as she had first seen him, sitting cross-legged, staring across the Ganges. The sun was just rising, and a finger of golden light shimmered on the water's surface as they tottered down the bank to the river's edge. The woman led her into the Ganges and pushed her head down. The cold water cleared her head and made her steadier on her feet, and, after changing into her dry sari, she felt able to start on the walk back to her village. The *sadhu* paid no attention to her departure. It was as though she had never been there.

By the time the next Holi came round the doctor at the local health centre had confirmed that Ram Lakhan's wife was carrying a child. Ram Lakhan made sure the whole village knew to avoid the humiliation he had suffered the year before, but he didn't

23

know whom to thank – the medicine man or Guru Gorakhnath. His wife knew that the baby had nothing to do with Gorakhpur, but she too wasn't entirely sure whether she should thank God or man.

Beyond Purdah

Suraiya was not a woman who liked to think that anyone had got the better of her, especially not domestic servants. The cooks who arrived in the household each year to prepare the evening meals during these ten days of Moharram always upset her. She knew they were cheats and that there was nothing she could do about it because the elder women of the family always defended them. But that didn't stop her dipping a ladle into the yellow-brown *kichara* – a gruel of several different types of grain and meat – bubbling vigorously in a smoke-blackened pot. She lifted the ladle and poured the liquid back slowly, leaving one small piece of meat in the bottom. Tasting it, she asked sharply, 'What sort of meat is this? It's still tough after cooking for five hours. The butcher must have given this goat away. It must have been born when my grandfather was young.'

The cook paid no attention. His colleagues, who were kneading great mounds of dough, peeling potatoes and preparing the *tandoors* in which the sweet, red-topped *roghani rotis*, the favourite bread of the family, would be baked, paid no attention either. Suraiya moved away, muttering to herself about thieving which got worse every year.

The sight in the pillared hall which formed the largest room of the main house didn't please her either. It was dusk and there was, as usual, an electricity cut. The hall was lit by the bright white light of hissing Petromax lamps. Almost every branch of the family of the late Taluqdar Taqi Miyan had come home for Moharram,

the most important occasion of their year. There were children
running wild, gossiping mothers, garrulous grannies and great-
grannies too. There seemed to be women everywhere. All wore
black or white mourning dress in memory of the martyrdom of
the Prophet Mohammad's grandson Imam Husain at the battle of
Karbala, but the atmosphere seemed anything but funereal. The
women still had plenty to talk about, even though they'd been
together for six days already. There was occasional laughter too,
although this was officially frowned on during the anniversary of
Imam Husain's martyrdom. Imam Husain had been killed at Karbala by the army of the man who claimed to be Caliph, or head
of the faith of Islam. The great schism in Islam between Shias
and Sunnis had sprung from this battle and the dispute over the
Caliphate.

'It's so typical of the lackadaisical ways of our Shia families,'
Suraiya thought. 'No wonder our fortunes have fallen so low when
these women just lie around gossiping as though nothing
had changed since the days their men prospered merely by
collecting rents from their lands. The way our men are going,
we won't have the money to finance these Moharram reunions
soon.'

Suraiya made her way across the crowded floor to a corner
where a group of slender young girls were standing practising one
of the laments which concluded the many *majlises*, or assemblies,
held during Moharram to mourn the martyrdom of Imam Husain.
Her daughter stood in the centre, holding a notebook of lyrics,
which the girls were reciting to a new tune they'd learned in
Victoria Street in Lucknow. As they chanted, they beat their chests
with their open palms in time to the metre of the verse.

Suraiya interrupted. 'That's enough, *beti*, get ready to go to the *majlis.* We must arrive before there's such a crowd there's no room for us.'

'We're just coming,' replied her daughter, launching into another verse.

Suraiya moved over to her husband's eldest aunt, who was lying against a cushion talking to another elderly woman. 'Bari Phuphi,' she said, 'they will listen only to you. Help me get everyone organized. We must leave for the Inner Village.'

The old lady took Suraiya's hand and said, 'Be patient. All in good time. When did we ever turn up to their *majlis* on time?'

Suraiya pulled her hand away impatiently and walked off. Bari Phuphi shook her head sadly, saying, 'What a pass we have come to. Look at that Suraiya – she has cut her hair, and now her husband, my nephew Asghar, doesn't even insist that she covers her head when she goes out. I remember the days when the men used to insist on strict *purdah*. Now they just sit around gossiping about their wretched politics.'

Munni Baji, an old lady with thick spectacles askew across her nose, spoke out with remarkable clarity, seeing that she didn't have a tooth in her head. 'They were much better days when there were no politics because of the British rule. Everyone talks about freedom but the freedom we have is destruction.' Getting into her stride, Munni Baji went on, 'That Suraiya, she's one of these new free women. They say they've freed us women, but I don't want their freedom. The fun we used to have when we had proper *purdah* – that was when we really enjoyed ourselves. There was so much happening in the house, so many friends, such a big family, so much fun, so much affection. We never had any work to do. We were never alone.'

Another elderly member of the family, wrapped in a shawl in   27 spite of the summer heat, agreed. 'Even the food doesn't taste the same now. Then we used to sit around the stove and eat. Chickens, whole goats, were slaughtered and cooked on cow dung, which really gives a taste. What sort of taste can you get sitting around a table?'

'And the prices! Then ten people could eat three meals for one silver rupee, now you get nothing for a bundle of one-hundred rupee notes. They're nothing more than dirty paper,' said Munni Baji.

Eventually Bari Phuphi called over to the girls, 'Come on, get ready to go. We are getting late for the *majlis*.'

One tradition which survived among the descendants of Taluqdar Taqi Miyan was obedience to Bari Phuphi, and so the women gathered in the courtyard.

Munni Baji grumbled, 'I suppose we have to walk all through the *basti* and cross that crowded bazaar, and down alongside that filthy pond where the butchers live. In the old days we weren't even allowed to cross to the house on the other side of the lane unless we were carried from one courtyard to another in a *doli*, with its sides curtained.'

Bari Phuphi replied irritably, 'I know. When my mother travelled by train, the whole carriage was reserved for her. All its windows were blacked out, and they used to put up a corridor of curtains on the platform so that no one could see her getting on to the train. But those days have gone, and now we just have to walk, so there's no point in grumbling.'

They walked in single file, all except Suraiya draped in black *burqas* which made them almost invisible in the limited light of a new moon. Nevertheless they hugged the side of the narrow lane to make themselves even more inconspicuous. They moved like ghosts across the main road, diving into the darkness behind the brightly lit stalls of the bazaar. As they approached the big house they held their noses to block the foul stench from the quarters of the village butchers. At the gate of the big house which had been built by Taluqdar Saddan Miyan two hundred years before, they found the great wooden gates had been left open for them. They crossed the courtyard and passed through what had once been the kitchens into the *zenana* or women's quarters. Grass and weeds were growing out of the crumbling walls which surrounded this courtyard. The roofs of all the rooms had fallen in except for one small hall used as an *imambara*, or house of the Imam, where tall *tazias*, replicas of the Imam's tomb made of bamboo and coloured paper, were arrayed. The hall was crowded with the women of the Inner Village's family and their neighbours.

The women descendants of Taluqdar Taqi Miyan clambered over the congregation of the *majlis*, who were sitting on the white sheets spread over the floor, listening intently to an elegy of the poet Anis. Suraiya tripped over a woman, who scolded, 'Is this any time to arrive? At least sometimes try to be punctual.' Eventually she squeezed herself in between two members of the other family. An elderly woman was sitting on a chair draped in black, reciting the poet Anis' description of the suffering of the women and infant children at Karbala, denied water by the Imam's enemies for many days. As the couplets told of the children's thirst, their hunger and their fear, her voice rose, and she rocked back and forth; sometimes looking down at her book to remind herself of the words, sometimes looking up at the congregation and from time to time dabbing the tears from her eyes with a lace handkerchief. When the elegy had ended the whole congregation stood

29

and a group of women chanted a lament, each verse ending with
the refrain

> Listen to the strains of mourning,
> See how cruelly heroes die.
> Homes are looted, camps are burning,
> Innocent children cry.

As the lament concluded, the women began to beat their breasts
in unison to cries of '*Ya* Husain! *Ya* Husain!', mourning the
martyred Imam. Their voices rose, the tempo quickened, reached
a climax, then suddenly died away. The *majlis* was over. Some
women sat down again, while others reached for their *burqas*. One
woman moved among the congregation distributing sweets which
had been blessed. Then the congregation dispersed.

Outside the hall a group of women belonging to Taluqdar
Saddan Miyan's family started to discuss the big *majlis* they had
attended with their menfolk that morning.

'The man who recited came all the way from Delhi again this
year.'

'Yes. He's a very important officer in the IAS.'

'He's a Hindu but that's good. It just shows that there's really
no enmity between us Shias and Hindus. It's the politicians who
cause all the problems.'

'In my grandfather's time a Kannauj Brahmin would come here
to recite.'

Suraiya, listening to the women boasting about their family's
majlis, became impatient. There was a traditional rivalry between
the two leading families of Mohammadpur. Each liked to claim
that their *majlis* had attracted the largest congregations and the
most important guests. Suraiya said in a loud voice, 'I suppose
your Pakistani relative made a big impact too?'

'Yes, he comes all the way from Karachi,' said one of the women.

'None of our family went to Pakistan at Partition,' replied Suraiya disdainfully.

'If someone went to Pakistan, that doesn't mean they are not members of the family. It's very right that they should come home for Moharram.'

'If they had such a great desire to go to Pakistan and break up their family, then they should stay there.'

By this time a small crowd had gathered and some were muttering against Suraiya, suggesting that if she wanted to insult their *majlis*, she and her whole family could stay at home. Bari Phuphi pulled Suraiya away, saying, 'Why are you always set on fighting? Learn a little self-control, a little modesty, a little sympathy for others. I don't know why Asghar doesn't control you.'

As they walked away Suraiya muttered, 'I don't see why we should sit down with Pakistanis when you are always saying it was the creation of that *kambakht* country which destroyed us.'

'You have so little understanding. Don't you know that the *majlis* doesn't belong to that Pakistani? It belongs to Imam Husain – every *majlis* does.'

Suraiya knew that in theory every *majlis* belonged to the Imam, but at the same time she also knew that a *majlis* reflected the status of a family. The Inner Gate family had done everything that Suraiya disapproved of. They had neglected their lands; they had allowed their home to fall into disrepair; they had in effect deserted Mohammadpur. But at the same time many of them had prospered in Lucknow, Delhi, Karachi and other big cities as lawyers, journalists and university teachers. They were able to come back for Moharram each year and resume their position as members of the leading Shia family, treating Suraiya's family like country 31 bumpkins. The smart Inner Village gentlemen from the cities showed no respect to her menfolk, although they were the ones who maintained the Shia presence in Mohammadpur throughout the year. What reward did her family get? They no longer had the rents from twenty villages to live on. They had to survive on the land left to them after the government had wreaked havoc by abolishing the *zamindari* system. What was worse, they couldn't possibly work the land themselves – that would have been beneath their dignity – and agricultural workers were now conscious of their rights. Their demands grew every year, but the fields didn't produce any more. Something would have to be done.

Shortly after Moharram the crisis broke. Asghar told Suraiya he was going to Azamgarh, the district headquarters, to see an agent about selling some of their land. His wife was horrified. 'That's all the capital we have,' she said.

'I have to pay our debts,' muttered her husband shamefacedly.

'That's the path to ruin. You sell first one field, run up more debts, then sell another until we have nothing left.'

'What else can I do? If I don't get this burden of interest off my back, the bank will take all our land anyhow.'

'I don't know what else you can do, but you will not sell one *bigha* of our land, that I promise you.'

Asghar shrugged his shoulders and walked away to join the men of the family sitting in the courtyard discussing the various *majlises* they had attended.

Suraiya sat for some time on her own, becoming more and more angry. Why were the men of her family so feckless? They took great pride in retaining the old feudal traditions, but they wouldn't lift a finger to provide the means to continue that way of life. Asghar himself had been quite successful in politics as long as the big leaders had valued his contacts, as a former landlord. But, like a fool, he had never made any money out of politics. He'd basked in the glory that his political contacts gave him. He'd been delighted when people said, 'Asghar is a big man. He can fix it for us.' But he'd regarded it as beneath the dignity of a Taluqdar to take money for the favours he did. What an idiot he'd been. Now politics had been taken over by the people the Taluqdars had always looked down on. Asghar was out.

Watching the men basking idly in the sun enraged Suraiya. She shouted to her husband, 'Come inside. I have something to say to you.'

The other men laughed. 'Go on, Asghar. The boss is calling you.'

'It's a good thing he's got a boss,' yelled Suraiya. 'Someone has to do something about you loafers. I'm going to see that there's at least one man in this family.'

Asghar got up and went indoors. His wife sat cross-legged on a wooden bed. He slumped into a chair and began to roll yet another cigarette.

'Do you want our family to be like the Inner Gate's?' she asked. 'Do you want our house to collapse like theirs?'

'No, of course I don't, but what can we do?'

'I'll tell you what we can do. You can go out and earn your living, start a business.'

'Business!' exclaimed Asghar, as though the proposal was preposterous.

'Yes, there's a clear path forward. Those crude contractors and their *goondas* have pushed you out of politics. They've decided they don't need you now that you've helped them make the money to buy votes. Now it's up to you to beat them at their own game.' 33

'What do you mean? That I should become a contractor?'

'Yes, just that.'

Asghar was appalled. 'That's ridiculous. Our family has never been in business. It's beneath our dignity, alien to our whole nature.'

'What will happen to your dignity if we have to spread our hands before others for money?' She paused, looked him straight in the eye and continued, 'If you won't go in for contracting, can you tell me what else you intend to do to save the family?'

Asghar couldn't believe his ears. It was bad enough having a wife who humiliated him in front of the other men of the family in the way Suraiya did, but if she was now going to start a campaign to get him into business, that would be intolerable. He stubbed out his cigarette, got up and walked out of the house saying, 'Now you've crossed all limits.'

'Just you see,' Suraiya shouted after him.

Suraiya beat her forehead with her hands in frustration. What could she do? There was no way of getting her husband to do anything. He would just sit around and watch the family go to ruin. She couldn't save them. It was unthinkable that a woman of Taluqdar Taqi Miyan's family should work. All she could think of doing was to seek advice outside the family.

Through Asghar's political work Suraiya had become friendly with Tara Ahmed, one of the few Muslim women who was prominent in the Congress Party. She arranged to meet her in Lucknow.

The leader lived in a large official bungalow in Mall Avenue. The security guard at the gate stopped Suraiya, saying, 'You can't come in without an appointment.'

'I know,' said Suraiya. 'That's why I have one.'

The security guard was taken aback. He had assumed that

Suraiya was just another of the hapless petitioners he took a delight in bullying. Without further questioning he let her in.

Tara Ahmed was not a politician who valued only those who could be useful to her. She had been fond of Asghar and had enjoyed coming to his home when she was in that area, so she welcomed Suraiya into her house.

When Suraiya explained her problem Tara Ahmed said, 'That's easy. Why don't we get Asghar back into politics? The Congress urgently needs help with the Muslim vote.'

'That wouldn't help,' replied Suraiya. 'He never made any money out of politics.'

'Why don't you go into politics?'

'Me?'

'Yes, you. I'm a Muslim woman, a wife, and I'm in politics, so why not you?'

'Asghar would never allow me to be seen in public making speeches and all that.'

Tara Ahmed tried to persuade her at least to consider politics, but Suraiya was adamant. She knew that was unrealistic, and she hadn't come all the way to Lucknow for advice which would not help her. Then Tara Ahmed suggested she should go into business. She promised to put opportunities her way and pointed out that business could be done from home. But Suraiya was still not convinced. If Asghar regarded it as beneath his dignity to be in business, what on earth would he say about his wife?

Tara Ahmed leant forward, took both Suraiya's hands in her own and said, 'I understand you, please believe that. But you know that there is nothing you can do with Asghar. He's never going to make money. Surely, then, you are the only one who can help? I remember the opposition I had from my family, but I overcame it because I was determined, and I have never regretted that. I promise you, from my own experience, it's only taking the decision that is hard. Very soon Asghar will come to accept it. If you are determined, he will have to.'

'Of course, you're right. If I don't do something, no one will. But what you are asking is very difficult. It goes against all the traditions of our family, and it's the family I'm trying to save.'

'I understand, but what won't a dying person do? At least go home and think about it, and remember that I can help you if you do decide to go ahead. Think of me as someone you can rely on for support in everything.'

Suraiya was moved by the politician's obvious affection for her. She trusted her. But she herself would be the one who had to take the decision and face the consequences, and she was far from convinced that she even wanted to flout the family traditions.

On the train journey back home Suraiya thought about the possibility of going into business. It was not her ability that worried her. It was all that she would have to surrender. She did not observe strict *purdah*. She had a reputation as a rebel in the family. But she was not really a rebel at all. She loved the family, all its branches, and she couldn't do anything which might cause a rift, like breaking away from the traditional role of a wife. Supposing, because of her, the family didn't all gather for Moharram next year? What would be the point of making money to save the family if the very way she earned the money destroyed it?

When Bari Phuphi ruled out the proposal that she should go into business, Suraiya thought that was the end of the matter. There could be no question of any woman in the family going against Bari Phuphi. It was unthinkable.

36   But the very next day a report of a shameful incident in the

bazaar reached Suraiya. Apparently a shop-keeper had abused Asghar, shouting at him about people who pretended to be aristocrats but in reality didn't have the money to pay their debts. A crowd had gathered and had grown quite hostile. Unfavourable comparison had been made with the Inner Village family members, who threw their money around when they came back for Moharram. Suraiya was livid. She went to look for her husband and found him, as usual, sitting with his cousins and friends in the courtyard. Forgetting all decorum, she stood over him and shouted, 'You never told me we owed money in the bazaar too!'

This was too much even for the mild Asghar. 'Don't you dare insult me in front of my friends,' he shouted back.

'I will insult you a lot more. Since you don't have the ability to provide for the family, I will. See how you like that.' And, turning on her heels, she walked away.

When she had calmed down Suraiya realized what she had done. She'd committed herself in front of all the family. If she now went back on her word, she would become a laughing-stock.

Then she thought, 'The words just seemed to come out of my mouth. I didn't really speak them myself. Maybe it was fate deciding for me. I can't say they were the words of God – it would be blasphemy – but maybe it was meant to happen.'

That thought, more even than the consequences of not carrying out her threat, gave Suraiya the strength to defy tradition.

A few weeks later Asghar was not a little concerned to observe Hukum Chand, the defeated Congress candidate in the last election, walk into the courtyard. He folded his hands politely in greeting to the men and asked whether Suraiya was in. The men pointed to the house.

After an hour or so the Hindu emerged with a broad smile on 37 his face, paid his respects again and walked off. He'd been delighted with the deal that Suraiya had offered. She would deliver Muslim votes to him if he helped her to become a contractor. Not only would that mean his political career would recover, but he would also be able to damage his opponent's business interests. Hukum Chand took contracts from the Public Works Department, which ruled him out of the Irrigation Department. That had become the virtual monopoly of his opponent, but now Suraiya would, he was sure, prove a formidable rival.

There was no difficulty in persuading the Irrigation Engineer that putting all his eggs in one basket did not make sound business sense, so he was the next visitor to invade what Asghar thought was his sanctuary – his home. The engineer arrived with an elderly man wearing a *dhoti* and silk *kurta*, whom he introduced as the *munshi*. He would provide and supervise the labourers for Suraiya's business. He would also make sure that no more work was done than was absolutely necessary to allow the engineer to certify that the contract had been completed. That would mean fat profits to be shared for all the work which should have been done but wasn't and for all the supplies which should have been supplied but weren't.

Before long there was a marked improvement in the family's finances, but naturally Asghar was not happy about this. Suraiya was an attractive woman, and perhaps this was the reason that the Irrigation Engineer and Hukum Chand found it necessary to call on her regularly. Asghar was kept out of their business meetings, but after they were over he found ashtrays full and glasses which smelt of cheap Indian whisky. Nothing could be kept a secret in Mohammadpur, and the *basti* was soon alive with rumours about drinking sessions and worse in Asghar's house where, until recently, no man outside their family circle had been allowed to enter.

The rumours crossed the road to the few inhabitants of the Inner Gate who still lived in the dilapidated ruins of their ancestral homes. Matters reached such a pass that the *maulvi* preached against the iniquity of unchaperoned women holding long meetings with men who weren't even Muslims. No name was mentioned, but the congregation at Friday prayers knew who the sinner was.

Eventually Bari Phuphi decided that a meeting of all the senior relatives living in Mohammadpur had to be called. The *maulvi* was invited too. He was a young man with a straggly beard and a small black bruise marking the place where his forehead touched the floor of the mosque five times a day in prayer. He'd qualified as an *alim*, an approved teacher and preacher, in Lucknow. In Bari Phuphi's younger days there had been no Shia *maulvi* in Mohammadpur. They had been called from Lucknow for special occasions, but elderly and pious Muslims had performed the ceremonies for the dead and for the earlier stages of life that the faithful passed through. Now the younger generation had lost this knowledge and, besides, Iranian money had considerably increased the number of young men passing out of theological colleges, all of whom needed employment.

Bari Phuphi would have preferred not to have this pious stranger interfering in what was a family matter. The *maulvi*, however, was too raw to appreciate the old lady's feelings and launched into a direct attack on Suraiya and Asghar too.

Suraiya cut him short, saying, 'I don't have any desire to hear myself insulted. It's up to God, not you, to judge me and my work. He has the contract for forgiveness, *sahib*, not you.'

One of the younger uncles put a hand over his mouth to stifle his laughter, but a more elderly relative protested, 'You shouldn't talk like that to the *maulvi*. Since he came here he has established an Islamic atmosphere in the *basti*. Many people come for Friday prayers, and he's right to protest when he finds sin spoiling that atmosphere.'

'Sin!' scoffed Suraiya. 'Can you only find sin in my house? Is everyone else washed with milk, they're so pure? Just look at the history of this family. Taqi Miyan didn't rule his villages by bothering about sin.'

Bari Phuphi was very unhappy about the way the meeting was going. Of course Suraiya should be censured and the family name protected, but this was not the way to do it. Without looking at the *maulvi*, she said, 'It's better that we discuss this within the family, Maulvi Sahib, if you would give us leave. This is not something you need to bother yourself with just now.'

The *maulvi* started to protest that it certainly was, but he was cut short by Suraiya, who said, 'In this family we listen to Bari Phuphi. You can go.'

Some of the men looked distinctly unhappy at this snub to the *maulvi*, but they said nothing. The man of God stood up, smoothed down his *kurta*, adjusted his round cap and walked out with his head held high. He was not going to let this insult to the dignity of his office pass. Suraiya was entirely wrong. He was entirely right. She must be punished.

Then Bari Phuphi took charge of the meeting. She spoke of the tradition of *purdah*, saying it was an honourable tradition which respected the modesty of women. It was mistaken to believe that women in *purdah* were oppressed. If she had been cowed, why was she so respected? When Suraiya said it was necessary for her to break *purdah* to save the family finances, Bari Phuphi had to agree that it was indeed a shame that her husband couldn't provide the wherewithal for the family to live as they should. However, she went on to say, even poverty has to be preferred to dishonour. Suraiya maintained that a woman could do business if her husband did not object. Everyone turned to look at Asghar, but he sat silently staring down at the floor.

'Please tell them,' said Suraiya. 'Do you object to my earning money?'

Asghar still did not reply. Bari Phuphi, exasperated by his weakness, said, 'I'm not surprised that Suraiya's running wild with a husband like that. He couldn't tether a goat, let alone control a frisky woman.'

'I didn't ask her to work,' mumbled Asghar. 'She insisted. She's my wife, but she's your niece. You arranged for me to marry her, so you control her.'

'I never thought I'd see a human being your size as helpless as an infant,' said Bari Phuphi. She reached for her stick, levered herself to her feet and, turning to Suraiya, said, 'You are the only man here.' Then she hobbled out of the room. The men dispersed without a word.

In his sermon on the next Friday the *maulvi* worked himself up into a lather of righteous indignation, inveighing against those who did not respect the learning of the clergy, women who practised immorality, men who allowed them to do so, defiance of God and many other grave, grave sins, all of which he knew would be ascribed to Suraiya. That evening two of the elders of the Taqi Miyan family went to the new house the faithful had built for the *maulvi* and implored him not to humiliate their family again. The *maulvi* was insistent. 'How can I allow such sin to go unpunished?'

he asked. 'It will undo all the good I've done in improving the atmosphere here.'

The elders had no answer to that. They were very pious themselves and thoroughly disapproved of all these goings-on. Assu Miyan rubbed the back of his bald pate and pleaded, 'Maulvi Sahib, we have thought and thought, but how can we do anything if Asghar doesn't take his wife in hand?'

'Compel him to. Threaten him.'

'To say that is one thing, but to do it another.'

'Suraiya is very fond of Moharram and proud of her *majlis* of the Eighth Day, I'm told.'

'That she is.'

'Well, tell her that you'll boycott her *majlis* next year. I'll make sure the Inner Village does.'

'It will be difficult for us to boycott the *majlis* of a member of our own family, and you know about our old rivalry with the Inner Village. But on a matter as great as this, I suppose we should be able to forget our differences.'

On their way home the two men passed three *burqa*-clad women making their way back from the bus stand.

'It's such a shame on us,' Assu Miyan said. 'In the old days the lower-caste families did not have the time to bother with *purdah*, nor the money either. Now they are the ones who are observing *purdah*, while our women are breaking it.'

'Yes,' replied his cousin, 'our family fought for independence in the Congress Party, but that same party destroyed us by taking our land away. It's the lower castes, who made no sacrifices for Independence, who have benefited from it. Now I wonder why we ever fought the British. We *zamindar* families were much better off under them.'

'But there's one thing, I tell you. Let the lower castes all wear *purdah*. It'll be generations before their women have the glow of genuine modesty on their cheeks, the glow our women have.'

The butchers were the other topic of conversation among the Shias of Mohammadpur. Someone had to sell meat to the carnivorous Muslims, but the trouble was that the Hindus would not allow the butchers to slaughter their buffaloes except in the privacy of their small houses. They couldn't sell the meat in the bazaar either. Customers had to come to the butchers' doors. This hadn't presented any problems as long as only rich Muslims could afford to eat meat regularly, but now almost everyone earned enough money to buy buffalo meat, and the number of butchers had increased to meet the demand. Unfortunately, their huts had sprung up on one side of a large pond in the middle of a *basti* of Shias and near the crumbling old house of the Inner Village family. The butchers chopped their meat on wooden stumps outside their huts. They piled up the bones in the corners of their yards and puddles of drying blood stained the ground. White scavenger vultures, their ruffs grubby with dust, kept the banks of the pond reasonably clean, but much of the butchers' waste found its way into the pond. The stench grew worse each summer.

Various efforts had been made to move the butchers to the outskirts of the small town. Land had even been offered to them, but they had refused to go. Although Muslims by faith, they were not notably pious, realizing that wealthier people regarded them with disdain, and so they were immune to threats from the *mullah* or pressure from the big families. They had played their politics cleverly, managing to offer their votes to the winner in the last State Assembly election, who now regarded them as a vote-bank 43 to be protected from attempts to move them. This meant the health hazard they represented went unremarked by any official.

The influential members of the family of the Inner Gate no longer lived in Mohammadpur and were not over-worried about the problems of the few cousins left behind. They kept a useful eye on the family mansion, but that was all. That was why it was not with any great expectations that Sajid, one of the cousins in Mohammadpur, wrote to his great-aunt, Asimun Dadi, informing her of the death of his young son. The boy had died of an undiagnosed illness which the doctor said had probably been caused by the unhygienic conditions of the neighbourhood. Sajid asked his great-aunt request her influential sons to have the butchers moved.

Asimun Dadi was staying in Delhi with her eldest son, Irfan, a lawyer in the Supreme Court, when Sajid's letter arrived. That evening she showed him the letter and asked what he was going to do about it.

'Why do you bother, *Amman*?' he replied. 'We don't have any real connection with Mohammadpur any longer, so why should we trouble with every branch of your vast family? Those days have passed.'

'They may have gone for you, *beta*, but Mohammadpur is still somewhere very special for me. If the conditions there are so unhealthy, no one will stay for Moharram, and that's the only time the family gets together. You are a lawyer. Why don't you file a case?'

'Where is the time? And then it wouldn't do any good.' Hoping that was the end of the matter, Irfan walked over to the sideboard and poured himself a whisky and soda.

His mother was a great traveller, moving around the country 44 staying with her many children. She was usually treated with the greatest respect wherever she went, but this was the one home where she knew she didn't count for much. Her eldest son was far too concerned about his career to bother about any relatives, and his wife practised in the Supreme Court too. The children had been sent to boarding schools in the foothills of the Himalayas. But the more Asimun Dadi was ignored, the more determined she became to make her presence felt. She walked over to the sideboard where Irfan was standing with that obstinate look she knew so well, took the glass from him, put it down and led him back to his chair. Smiling gently, she asked, 'Do I often demand anything from you? I taught you religion and customs, so that you would know what they were. But after that I left you free to decide your own course in life, to adapt to the age you live in, didn't I?'

'You have been very tolerant, *Amman*, I agree,' acknowledged Irfan.

'Has it ever been the women of this family who have been opposed to change? Didn't your grandmother support your uncle when he wanted to be in films and your father said he must go into government service? When he first acted in a film, your grandfather refused to see it, but your grandmother told him, "You don't know what a great man my son is. If he has done something, it will be very good." She even went to a public cinema to see the film!'

'I know,' said Irfan irritably, 'and now you will tell me how you came out of *purdah* so that you could choose our school and make sure we were being taught well, but –'

'Yes,' interrupted the old lady, getting into her stride, 'and the whole family rose up in protest against me. I was told I was going English, that my children would grow up knowing nothing of their religion, that I was immoral. But if I hadn't stood up to that 45 pressure, you wouldn't be here in Delhi with your smart house, your Supreme Court and your beautiful wife. You'd be back in Mohammadpur – a pauper trying to maintain the style of a Taluqdar.'

Irfan held up his hands to stem the torrent of words. 'All right, *Amman*, all right. When we go for Moharram this year I will see what can be done.'

'You must do, otherwise the whole family will be scattered for ever. When everyone hears about that poor child dying and sees the filth and dirt, they will run away as if rats had taken over the place and plague had come. It will be just like Delhi in the last rains, when the plague rumour spread – everyone went mad. This year Moharram comes at the height of the hot weather, and that pond will stink.'

Asimun Dadi always went to Mohammadpur with her brother a few days before the rest of the family arrived for Moharram to make sure the few habitable parts of the old house were clean and that the kitchen was prepared for the cooks. That year she took her eldest son Irfan too.

It wasn't easy to keep anything secret in Mohammadpur, so Irfan soon heard of the plan to boycott Suraiya's *majlis*. He was not surprised therefore that one of the first who called to pay his respects to the family was the *maulvi*. Bowing obsequiously and salaaming, he asked after the welfare of various members of the family. Irfan called for two chairs to be brought out on to the patchy grass of the courtyard under the shade of a *neem* tree. Inviting him to sit down, Irfan said, 'I believe, Maulvi Sahib, that we have something to discuss.' It would have been polite for Irfan to engage the *maulvi* in small talk at least until the inevitable cups of tea were brought out, but he was in no mood for such formalities.

'I have heard that you want us to boycott Suraiya's *majlis*,' he went on.

The *maulvi* had been hoping to introduce the subject with a long prologue on the sinfulness of Suraiya and the disrepute she was bringing on the Shia community. He had been convinced that his eloquence and the monstrosity of her sins would convince Irfan that something had to be done. But he was put out by Irfan's direct approach and his well-planned strategy deteriorated into a nervous gabble. 'Yes, yes. You see, it's very bad, really very bad. She's behaving very badly. We are all getting a bad name. My work, which is so important, is suffering. It looks bad if I can't stop her. Already the Sunnis are laughing at us behind our backs.'

Irfan checked the torrent of words, saying, 'I know, Maulvi Sahib. I agree it's most undesirable. My mother also feels she's gone too far, but there is one problem – our family is most likely leaving Mohammadpur for good.'

'Leaving!' said the *maulvi*, sitting bolt upright in his chair. 'That's not possible.'

'What is not possible in this world, Maulvi Sahib?'

'But why?'

'Because the filth is beyond endurance. The stench from that pond, produced by all the carrion left by the butchers, comes right up to here.'

'You are quite correct, of course. I have been trying to persuade them to go, but they are Sunnis, and they don't listen to me. They don't even follow their own *maulvi*. What can I do?'

'If you can't do anything, there won't be any members of my family here to boycott Suraiya's *majlis*. They'll all run when they see the conditions here. One child has already died. I am trying to persuade my mother to leave because I fear for her health.'

If the prominent visitors from the Inner Village deserted Mohammadpur for good, the consequences would be far more serious than just the collapse of the *maulvi*'s plan to punish Suraiya. It would be a major blow to the Shias, unbalancing the delicate relationship between the different communities of Mohammadpur. They would be reduced to an irrelevance, leaving them at the mercy of the Sunnis and Hindus. The Inner Village family had been the more important of the two Taluqdar families of Mohammadpur. It didn't matter that the lethargic Jaffar Miyan, who had been Taluqdar at the time of independence, had given away most of the family land. Birth, not wealth, granted prestige, and there was no doubt that the family of the Inner Village was still regarded by all communities in Mohammadpur as the leading family. This gave the Shias far more clout than their numerical position justified. Also, of course, it enhanced the *maulvi*'s prestige, although families of the Inner Village had never been great patrons of the clergy.

'But what have the butchers to do with me?' asked the *maulvi*.

'Quite simple,' replied Irfan briskly, making clear that, as far as he was concerned, the interview was over, 'You get rid of them and you have your boycott.'

The *maulvi* couldn't let matters rest there. 'You have the influence,' he pleaded. 'You live in Delhi. You have the *sifarish* with the big people. I'm merely a simple *maulvi*, living on the alms of the community.'

'It's not usual to find a *mullah* who is so humble,' replied Irfan in mock surprise. 'You people claim the right to rule nowadays, so rule.' Then, standing up, he bid the *maulvi* farewell and walked back to the house.

The *maulvi*'s head was bowed as he hurried back to his allies in the Taqi Miyan family. He didn't notice the crow-pheasant, with rust-red wings shining in the bright sunlight, strutting across the ground in front of him. 'Something has to be done quickly. Moharram is almost upon us,' he thought. He ignored the greetings of the women spinning outside the huts where their men sat weaving, their looms clacking with so many different noises it sounded as though every part must be going in a different direction and the whole must surely fall apart. 'I face a double disaster,' the *maulvi* muttered. 'All the work I have done will be destroyed, and my face will be blackened with disgrace.' The sound of the *azaan* from the new Sunni mosque didn't this time prompt him to hurry back to his own mosque for prayers. He went straight to the house of the most trusted elder of the Taqi Miyan family.

The elder gathered the men of the family together. The *maulvi*'s news shocked them deeply. Although there was little love lost between the two former ruling families, Taqi Miyan's descendants knew how damaging it would be for the whole Shia community if the Inner Village was deserted. But what could they do?

One of the elders said, 'They have the brains. That's why they have been able to earn their bread in the cities, and that's why they don't care about Mohammadpur. Our problem is that we have never been good at using our brains. We have always fought with our *lathis*.'

Bari Phuphi, who had joined the conclave, remarked sourly, 'You can't even do that nowadays – Suraiya is stronger than any one of you.'

'You are boycotting her *majlis*. God forbid you should suggest approaching that sinner for help,' said the by now thoroughly alarmed *maulvi*.

'But she's the one with the political strength now,' Bari Phuphi said. 'She could probably get the butchers moved.'

The *maulvi* tugged at the lobes of his ears, saying, '*Tauba! Tauba!* God forbid that anyone should suggest such a thing.'

No one had any alternative, so the meeting broke up. The *maulvi* was grateful that he'd managed to head off any suggestion of asking for Suraiya's help or lifting the embargo on her *majlis*, but he was deeply worried. The departure of the Inner Village still threatened to deal an even bigger blow to the prestige of the Shia community and to his own standing.

Suraiya soon heard of this new development. Although no one was prepared to ask for her help, she saw no reason why she shouldn't offer it. Here, perhaps, was a chance to get her own back on the men of the family and that wretched *maulvi* who had persuaded them to shame her. She walked through the narrow lanes where the Taqi Miyan family lived and across the main street. When she reached the huge wooden entrance to the Inner Gate, she found it closed and the elderly watchman leaning against it, fast asleep. She woke him with the abrupt command, 'Tell Irfan Sahib I have come to see him.'

Looking up, the watchman saw Suraiya standing over him, wearing a smart dark-green *salwar qamiz*.

'What did you say?' he asked in surprise. 'Who do you want to see?'

'I've told you: Irfan Sahib. Open the gate.'

This woman has no shame, thought the watchman. Coming here dressed like that and asking to see one of the men of the family. But he didn't want to pick a fight because he knew she came from a big family too, so he got to his feet, pulled back the
50 bolt and opened the gate. Irfan was sitting in the courtyard and,

to the watchman's surprise, got up to greet Suraiya as he saw her coming through the gateway. He led her on to the roof of the house, which overlooked some bedraggled guava trees, beds of summer vegetables and a dried-up well, all that remained of the family estates. 'You see this land?' said Irfan. 'We are thinking of selling it and knocking down the *haveli* because we can't keep it up. Many of us live away from here, and we can't maintain it.'

'Yes,' said Suraiya, 'I had heard that you want to leave Mohammadpur altogether.'

'News travels fast.'

'It's my business to know what's happening.'

Irfan was impressed, as Suraiya had been determined he should be. He spent so little time in Mohammadpur he might not have heard of her new-found power. He had to be convinced that she could deliver the bargain she was about to offer.

Suraiya spelt out that bargain in simple terms. Contractors financed politicians, so she now had considerable influence. She would use that influence to get the butchers moved from the pond, but only if Irfan and his family would come to her *majlis*.

'It won't be such easy work, you know, Suraiya. The MLA is backing the butchers.'

'What do you think will weigh more heavily with him – a few butchers' families or the women's vote?'

'But, according to the *maulvi*, all the women want you locked up.'

Suraiya laughed. 'What do you think the *maulvi* knows about women? He says they break *purdah* if they even look at him or any other man. I've learned one thing from being a contractor. There are two ways to get things done – one through heat and force and another through softness. It's the second that gives satisfaction. I have learned how to win people over using softness. Obviously, I don't have physical strength or bands of thugs, but I'm still a success.'

Irfan had a sneaking sympathy for Suraiya but, like a good lawyer, he demanded a foolproof guarantee before accepting her deal. She pointed out that he would have to trust her because there was no way of having the butchers moved out before Moharram. Not even she could make the government machinery move that fast. Realizing that he'd met his match but unwilling to acknowledge it, Irfan said that he would have to think the matter over.

Come Moharram Suraiya had still not heard anything from Irfan. The *maulvi* had no confirmation that the Inner Village family still intended to boycott Suraiya's *majlis*, but that didn't stop him informing her family that they did. With difficulty the men of Taq Miyan's family had persuaded Bari Phuphi that she must abide by the boycott too. She eventually agreed because she could see no other way of bringing Suraiya back to the path of orthodoxy.

Suraiya gave the impression that she didn't care. On the evening before the *majlis* was due to take place in their *imambara*, her husband Asghar pleaded with her. 'There's still time to change your mind. Just say you'll give up your contracting and everyone will come to our *majlis*. If they don't, we will never be able to live down the shame. We'll have to leave the *basti*.'

'Will you take over the contracting then?' asked Suraiya.

'You know I can't.'

'All right. Then I'll learn to live with the disgrace they want to pile on my head – even though they should have looked at the dirt inside their own collars before criticizing me. I have spent my life in this village and I know very well what they all get up to. In any case, I don't eat their bread and am not answerable to them. If they want to waste their time worrying over me, let them. I'll not waste my time on them. Instead I'll use it to do my work.'

But for all her bravado Suraiya was very distressed. She feared that Irfan's silence meant he had rejected her offer and would boycott the *majlis*. She had begun to question the point of upsetting everyone so much. Her aim had been to earn enough to preserve the honour of her house and to allow them to stay in Mohammad-pur with everyone acknowledging their status. If she was to be ostracized, she might as well forget Mohammadpur and go to the district headquarters, where she could continue her work much more conveniently. There, however, she would be no one very much, and certainly her family would count for nothing. She belonged in Mohammadpur.

The next morning her worst fears were confirmed. She sat waiting in the *imambara* for the congregation to join the renowned *alim* they had called from Lucknow, but only a few Hindu women had come to ask for favours from the *tazias* laid out in preparation for the great procession which was the culmination of Moharram. The whirring of two electric pedestal fans, circulating heat, was the only sound that broke the silence. Suraiya pulled the dividing curtain aside to see that the men's space was almost empty. There was only the *alim*, her husband and one or two family servants. The *alim* began to argue with Asghar, asking why he'd been brought all the way to Mohammadpur when there was no one to listen to him. He could have been addressing a mighty congregation somewhere else. There was no shortage of demand for his eloquence. Asghar knew that to be true by the fee he'd had to pay. Suraiya came from behind the *purdah* and tried to persuade the *alim* to stay, but this just made him more angry, '*Begum*,' he said, 'I was speaking with your husband. Return to your place.' Thereupon the *alim*   53 gathered together his books, adjusted his immaculate turban and rose to depart.

At that moment the door of the *imambara* was pushed open and in walked Irfan, followed by the entire male contingent of the Inner Village. Without saying a word, they sat down reverentially and waited for the *majlis* to start. The spy from the Taqi Miyan family, who had been watching the door of the *imambara* from behind a weaver's hut, moved off as fast as his dignity would allow to report this development to the men of the other branches of the family. There was consternation among them.

'Fools,' said Bari Phuphi as soon as the news reached her. 'Now it's we who are shamed, not Suraiya. Imagine what we will look like if we boycott a *majlis* of our own family and the Inner Village attend it.'

'But you agreed to the plan,' said one of her relatives querulously.

'Yes, and you said the Inner Village had too.'

Another cousin suggested that they call the *maulvi* to consult him. But he was told the clergyman had gone to a *majlis* in a neighbouring village. Bari Phuphi exploded. 'That wretched *maulvi*! Leave him to his own devices. He has drawn us into this mess. We should never let an outsider interfere in our family affairs.' Then she stood up. 'You may do as you like,' she announced. 'We women are going to the *majlis*.'

Later that afternoon the *maulvi* called to inquire after the success of the boycott. A grim-faced Bari Phuphi told him, 'It was a very splendid *majlis*. The *imambara* was packed full. There wasn't room to put a sesame seed.'

'I would never have expected this of you,' burst out the *maulvi*. 'You have let your religion down. You have let me down.'

'Perhaps we have,' replied Bari Phuphi, 'but perhaps that will teach you to keep within certain limits. I never saw the need for a *maulvi* in Mohammadpur. For generations we had all been quite able to look after ourselves.'

On the tenth day of Moharram, the anniversary of Imam Husain's martyrdom, the men of Taqi Miyan's family, joined by sundry other poorer Shias, took the *tazias* out of the *imambara*. The flimsy bamboo structures wobbled precariously on the mourners' shoulders as they marched down the narrow lanes. Many of the houses lining them had been replastered with cow dung and mud for Moharram. Hindu women poured water from small pots on to the ground as the procession approached – their offering of respect for the martyrs who had died thirsting. At the head of the procession Asghar and his cousins took it in turns to chant laments, and the refrains were picked up by the black-shirted young men behind them who were beating their chests in time to the metre. They beat themselves so hard that blood stained their shirts. All the rest of Mohammadpur, Hindus and Muslims, wealthy and poor, men and women, seemed to have left their homes, their shops, their fields and their businesses, to watch the *tazias* pass by in solemn mourning of the martyrdom of Imam Husain.

Occasionally the procession halted for a fragment of poetry to be chanted or to disentangle one of the taller *tazias* caught in overhead wires. When they reached the Inner Village, the men of Saddan Miyan's family, their followers and their *tazias* joined the procession. They all moved on through the lines of spectators to a small square. There they halted. A group of young boys, none older than eleven or twelve, bare-breasted and wearing white trousers, started to flail their backs. The thongs of their whips were chains, not leather. The tips were knives, not knots. The chanting became more and more frenzied. Men pressed in on all sides to see the blood oozing from the cuts on the boys' bare backs and to sprinkle rosewater on their wounds. The more pain the boys inflicted on themselves, the more ecstatic they became.

Irfan noticed Suraiya among the women standing on the steps of the mosque watching this frenzy. She saw him approaching, sheltering from the blistering sun under an umbrella, and called out, '*Arre,* Irfan *bhai*, you town people are so precious you don't want the sun to darken your skins.'

The women covered their mouths to hide their smiles. Irfan put down the umbrella and said, 'Well, it's been a good Moharram after all, Suraiya. I have kept my part of the deal. What about yours?'

'You go back to Delhi, where you belong,' replied Suraiya. 'Leave me to look after Mohammadpur.'

PENGUIN 60s

READ MORE IN PENGUIN

For complete information about books available from Penguin and how to order them, please write to us at the appropriate address below. Please note that for copyright reasons the selection of books varies from country to country.

IN THE UNITED KINGDOM: Please write to *Dept. EP, Penguin Books Ltd, Bath Road, Harmondsworth, Middlesex UB7 oDA.*

IN THE UNITED STATES: Please write to *Consumer Sales, Penguin USA, P.O. Box 999, Dept. 17109, Bergenfield, New Jersey 07621-0120.* VISA and MasterCard holders call 1-800-253-6476 to order Penguin titles.

IN CANADA: Please write to *Penguin Books Canada Ltd, 10 Alcorn Avenue, Suite 300, Toronto, Ontario M4V 3B2.*

IN AUSTRALIA: Please write to *Penguin Books Australia Ltd, P.O. Box 257, Ringwood, Victoria 3134.*

IN NEW ZEALAND: Please write to *Penguin Books (NZ) Ltd, Private Bag 102902, North Shore Mail Centre, Auckland 10.*

IN INDIA: Please write to *Penguin Books India Pvt Ltd, 706 Eros Apartments, 56 Nehru Place, New Delhi 110 019.*

IN THE NETHERLANDS: Please write to *Penguin Books Netherlands bv, Postbus 3507, NL-1001 AH Amsterdam.*

IN GERMANY: Please write to *Penguin Books Deutschland GmbH, Metzlerstrasse 26, 60594 Frankfurt am Main.*

IN SPAIN: Please write to *Penguin Books S. A., Bravo Murillo 19, 1° B, 28015 Madrid.*

IN ITALY: Please write to *Penguin Italia s.r.l., Via Felice Casati 20, I-20124 Milano.*

IN FRANCE: Please write to *Penguin France S. A., 17 rue Lejeune, F-31000 Toulouse.*

IN JAPAN: Please write to *Penguin Books Japan, Ishikiribashi Building, 2-5-4, Suido, Bunkyo-ku, Tokyo 112.*

IN GREECE: Please write to *Penguin Hellas Ltd, Dimocritou 3, GR-106 71 Athens.*

IN SOUTH AFRICA: Please write to *Longman Penguin Southern Africa (Pty) Ltd, Private Bag X08, Bertsham 2013.*